Loretta Santini

CITIES OF ITALY

ORVIETO

GUIDE WITH PLAN

Distributed by:
SOLINI MARCELLO
VIA LOGGIA DEI MERCANTI, 23
TEL. 341287 - ORVIETO

CENTRO STAMPA EDITORIALE
plurigraf
PERSEUS

ORVIETO

The tourist who arrives in Orvieto by rail or by road will see the town rising in the distance, set amid a beautiful landscape of fields and vineyards, and superbly situated on top of a volcanic outcrop, whose precipitous walls encircle it like a fortress dominating the broad valley of the river Paglia.

Due to its position, its Etruscan antiquities, the partly medieval appearance of its streets and above all its famous Cathedral, a jewel of Gothic art, Orvieto is one of the most fascinating towns in Italy.

An important Etruscan city, identified by some with Volsinii Veteres (or also Urbisvetus, old town, in contradistinction to Volsinii-novi, the neighbouring Bolsena), Orvieto also maintained its thriving economy in Roman times, based especially on the production of pottery.

During the barbarian invasions, Orvieto was occupied by Alaric and Odoacer. Vitigis, in turn, exploited its strong natural position to turn it into a defensive bastion in his war against the Byzantines under Belisarius, who succeeded in conquering it after a stubbornly-resisted siege in 538.

Temporarily reoccupied by Totila before the final Gothic defeat, Orvieto was later occupied by the Lombard Agilulf in 596. The town was granted its own bishop and, in 606, its own counts. A count of Orvieto, Farolf, as part of the religious revival promoted by the emperor Otto III, cooperated with St. Romuald in fostering the foundation of abbeys and monasteries in the surrounding territory.

In the 11th-12th century Orvieto set itself up as a Commune. The first towers, tower-houses and mansions of the nobility that moved from the countryside into the town began to arise. The Commune later rebelled against the papal governors installed to control it and engaged in lengthy struggles until it was finally recognised by Pope Hadrian IV.

By 1137 Orvieto had already become an independent city-state and speedily became a prominent Guelph stronghold in Central Italy, repulsing the repeated attacks of Ghibelline exiles and the Hohenstaufen emperors Frederick I and Henry IV.

The papal nomination of the first podestà (chief magistrate), the Roman Pietro Parenzo, dates to 119; he was later killed during the internecine strife between the opposing factions of the Monaldeschi (Guelphs) and Filippeschi (Ghibellines) which continued unabated throughout the 13th century. In 1281-84, the French Pope Martin IV established himself in Orvieto, filling the town with his own fellow-citizens, against whom the people rebelled. On the rekindling of civil strife, the Filippeschi were expelled from the town in August 1313. But their rivals, the Monaldeschi, became themselves divided into the opposing Beffati and Malcorini factions. In 1334 civil unrest was quelled by Ermanno Monaldeschi della Cervara, who became Orvieto's first Lord and ruled it until his death in 1337.

A few years later, in 1354, Cardinal Albornoz occupied the town and annexed it to the papal state. Orvieto, however, preserved its

communal institutions and liberties. In the following centuries it combined a measure of independence with the dignity of capital of the fifth province of the papal state, one it retained until 1798. After the Napoleonic interlude, Orvieto was incorporated in the delegation of Viterbo and in 1831 once again became capital of the province until being annexed by the Italian State in 1860. Orvieto's singular geographical position has made it a naturally fortified town. It has consequently never been surrounded by defensive walls.

Many archaeological remains testify to the existence of Etruscan and Roman monuments in the town and its immediate environs. Of the town's surviving medieval heritage, many fortified town-houses and several churches testify to the Romanesque style. The Gothic style – initially combined with the Romanesque – begins to emerge in the mid-14th century. It was during this period that Orvieto gave birth to the master-mason Master Angelo, the builder of the Palazzo Pubblico in Città di Castello and the Palazzo dei Consoli in Gubbio. Painting in the town had already been developed as early as the 13th century with the frescoes in San Giovenale and in the Abbey of Saints Severo and Martirio.

In the 14th century it was the Sienese school of painting which dominated in Orvieto with works by Simone Martini and Lippo Memmi, which determined the emergence of the local painters Ugolino di Prete Ilario, Giovanni di Buccio Leonardelli and Pietro di Puccio.

The Renaissance was represented in Orvieto – albeit belatedly – by Antonio Federighi.

In the 16th century Orvieto was the birthplace of artists of considerable value such as Ippolito Scalza, the sculptor and architect, his son Francesco and Ascanio Vittozzo. Thanks to the wealth of its artistic heritage, the characteristic products of its arts and crafts and the wine for which it is justly so famous, Orvieto is today one of the major tourist resorts in Central Italy, well-equipped with modern hotel facilities and a wide choice of excellent restaurants.

FIRST ENCOUNTER WITH ORVIETO

The tufa outcrop, on whose flat plateau Orvieto stands, rises like an island in the broad and level Paglia Valley.

The rock cliffs which surround it are precipitous and provide it with a natural fortification.

The town extends for the most part over the central part of the plateau, since, with the exception of one or two monasteries, it has never been permitted to build right on the edge of the rock-face.

The old town is characterized by narrow, winding streets, flanked by low and irregular houses which form, at every turning, ever new und unexpected picturesque views.

The panorama of Orvieto is especially lovely when seen from afar, as when the visitor first glimpses it from the winding Umbro-Casentinese road, on an autumn morning, when the faint mist gathered along the valley floor has not yet completely dissolved: Orvieto then seems like a great battleship floating above the foaming waves, and its cliffs, towers and Cathedral form a picture of rare beauty.

Equally inviting is the panorama of Orvieto on a fine summer day, when the great rocky bluff on which it so proudly stands is more clearly silhouetted against the blue sky, dominated by the Cathedral, and its roofline fretted by the church and belfry of San Francesco, the Torre del Moro, the Papal Palace and the Palazzo del Capitano del Popolo.

THE TOWN

Almost at the centre of the built-up area of Orvieto, towards the west, is the Piazza del Comune, now known as the Piazza della Repubblica. Historians of Orvieto agree that this square occupies the site where once the Etruscan, and later Roman, forum stood; it was traversed longtitudinally by the decumanus (the main east-west thoroughfare), represented by an irregular line now followed by the Corso Cavour, the Piazza della Repubblica and the Via della Cava. On the south side of the Piazza stands the **Palazzo Comunale**, built over the remains of the previous town hall, whose slender Gothic arcades supporting the roof are still preserved in the second storey. Designed by the local architect Ippolito Scalza, the building was begun in 1573 and finished – though not completely – in 1582.

Four arches are still lacking on the west side of the façade. The arch flanked by two coupled columns was supposed to have been at the centre of the ten arcades and to have formed the principal entrance, whereas today it is situated, at the opening of the fourth arcade to the right, in the Via Garibaldi. This beautiful piazza is flanked to the east by the church of Sant'Andrea with its battlemented twelve-sided bell-tower and its portico entirely restored in 1930. On the left side of the church of Sant'Andrea begins the Corso Cavour, which cuts longitudinally through the southern part of Orvieto from the Piazza della Repubblica to the Piazzale Cahen. The Corso is embellished with numerous ancient palaces, especially prominent being the one known as the "Palazzo dei Sette" (Palace of the Seven). This building (the Palazzo dei Sette), was erected in the 13th century at the same time as the square tower by which it is flanked. Originally owned by the Della Terza family, it later be-

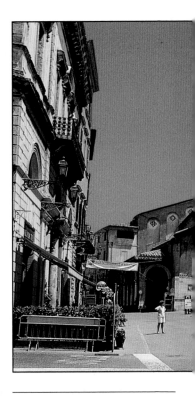

Above: *Piazza della Repubblica.*
Below right: *Palazzo Comunale.*

came the property of the Commune, before being transferred to the Caetani family and then to the Holy See and eventually being returned to the Commune in 1516 – the gift of Pope Leo X – as the official residence of the papally-appointed Governors and Apostolic Delegates.

To the left of the Palazzo rises the tall tower known as the **Torre del Moro**. Originally the tower of the Della Terza family, it was called the Torre del Papa (The Pope's Tower) until the 17th century, because it formed part of the Papal Palace. It later became known as the Torre del Moro or Torre del Saracino (the Moor's òr Saracen's Tower), because a Saracen's head targe was attached to it which medieval knights used to tilt

The Mancinelli Theatre.

against with their lance during the horse-back tournaments known as the "Quintana": a competitive event which is still celebrated in period costumes in several towns in Umbria and Tuscany. The tower is 42 metres high and the bell which strikes the hours bears the coats of arms of the 24 Guilds that contributed to the cost of its casting in 1316. Continuing along the Corso Cavour, we find, to the right, the **Teatro Comunale** dedicated to the local musician L. Mancinelli. The building in which the theatre is housed was designed by the Perugian architect Giovanni Santini, and built in 1844 on the site of the former Palazzo Orienti. Work on its construction having been suspended, it was only resumed eleven years later with new plans supplied by Virginio Vespignani. The elegant interior consists of four rows of boxes and a balcony. The large drop-curtain, entirely painted by the local painter Cesare Fracassini, depicts an important military episode in the history of Orvieto: «Belisarius liberating Orvieto from the Goths» (535). The central ball-room is decorated with paintings of the Four Seasons. After over ten years of restoration work, the Mancinelli Theatre was restored to the public, completely refurbished, in December 1993.

PIAZZA DEL POPOLO

Orvieto's biggest piazza is the Piazza del Popolo. It is dominated by the imposing Palazzo del Capitano del Popolo, on which particular beauty is conferred by the warm golden colour assumed over the centuries by the soft vulcanic stone (tufa) with which it is entirely built.

Originally built as a papal palace during the pontificate of Hadrian IV (*ca.* 1157), it is in the Orvietan Romanesque-Gothic style and consists of an open loggia on the ground floor and a large council-hall on the first floor. Later the Church granted it to the Commune as the seat of the Captain of the People. And to make it habitable on the eastern side, above the triumphal staircase, a room (called the "Caminata") was added, its exterior imitating the motif of the round triple-arched mullioned windows of the large hall. In 1280, furthermore, a bell-tower was added at the building's eastern end, while to the west the council hall was altered to give it its present appearance.

Following the subsequent closure of the arcades of the ground-floor loggia, the two pointed arches were opened to form the so-called "Arco della Pesa". A modern restoration carried out by the architects Paolo and Carlo Zampi has restored the building to its original appearance.

The Palazzo del Capitano del Popolo (Palace of the Captain of the People) has been completely restructured inside, including its interesting "Hall of the Four

Torre del Moro.

Hundred", to serve as a congress centre.

The restoration work carried out on the monument has decidedly enhanced its historical value, while at the same time responding to the needs of a modern congress centre.

The semi-circular arches over the windows are decorated with pierced rosettes and framed by a broad chequerboard moulding of cubes cut into the tufa. The building is topped by a crenellated roofline.

From the top of its external staircase of from its windows a marvellous view can be enjoyed of the picturesque market held in the Piazza on Thursday and Saturday mornings.

Facing the Palazzo del Capitano del Popolo is the **Palazzo Bracci**, designed by Virgilio Vespignani and now converted into a first-class hotel, and the Romanesque **Church of San Rocco**, with frescoes painted by the school of Signorelli and Cristoforo da Marsciano (1527).

The Palazzo del Capitano del Popolo.
Below right: Three mullioned windows of the Palazzo del Capitano del Popolo.
Below: Interior of the Church of San Rocco.

THE CATHEDRAL

In 1263/4 a Bohemian priest – a certain Peter of Prague – incredulous about the trans–substantiation of the Body and Blood of Christ in the Host and the Wine, went on a pilgrimage to Rome to pray at the tomb of St. Peter for the strengthening of his faith.

On the return journey from Rome, he stopped at Bolsena where, on celebrating Mass in the crypt of Santa Cristina, he saw blood dripping from the Host, so much so that the Corporal – the eucharistic altar cloth – was quite soaked with it. Pope Urban IV, who was then in Orvieto, was so impressed by this miraculous event that he ordered the linen cloth to be transported there and later established the Feast of Corpus Christi for the whole Christian world. The clergy and people agreed that a worthy shrine should be built to house the Relic.

And on 13 November 1290 Pope Nicholas IV laid the foundation stone of the new church. The place chosen for it was the one already occupied bu the churches of San Costanzo and Santa Maria Prisca.

Work on the construction of the Cathedral was protracted for roughly three centuries. The first architect was probably Arnolfo di Cambio: to him has also been attributed the design for a single-gabled façade preserved in the Cathedral Museum. It seems, however, that the first master-mason responsible for the Cathedral's construction was Fra Bevignate da Perugia who built the nave and side aisles. The work was then continued by a local builder, Giovanni Uguccione, who introduced the Gothic style in the crossing and the apse. Right from the outset, however, the stability of the Cathedral's principal load-bearing structures was in doubt, with the result that it was decided to call in an expert to give his view.

The Sienese architect and sculptor Lorenzo Maitani was the man chosen. He not only ensured the stability of the dangerous transepts by the buttresses he himself designed (1309-10), but delighted the citizens of Orvieto with his coloured design for a triple-gabled façade to the new church. With the construction of the façade he also began and pursued that of the roof. Before his death, Maitani had left his architectural impress not only on the façade, but also on the interior of the church, such as the construction of the tribune over the wings of the eastern buttresses, a masterpiece of elegance and harmony which he completed by his Gothic transformation of the Sanctuary. The building of the tribune was finished after Maitani's death in Orvieto in June 1330.

The Cathedral - The façade.

14

THE BAS-RELIEFS

The Cathedral façade is composed of four polygonal piers, two at the sides and two at the centre (with higher pinnacles). These divide the surface of the façade into a tripartite scheme corresponding, in the interior, to the nave and two aisles. The four piers have a marble revêtement at their base, forming four pilasters which are decorated with exquisite bas-reliefs. No absolute certainty exists about the identity of the sculptors who produced these masterpieces of 14th century art.

Some scholars think that the bas–reliefs of the inner pilasters are earlier. Yet the best of the reliefs are usually attributed to Maitani. There are devoted to scenes illustrating the origins of man, the mystery of Redemption and man's ultimate destiny.

Above the pilasters, and between the portals, four bronze statues representing the emblems of the Evangelists are placed over a finely moulded cornice running horizontally across the façade.

They are: the Man-Angel (St. Matthew), the Lion (St. Mark), the Eagle (St. John) and the Winged Bull (St. Luke).

Presumably dating to *ca.* 1329, these statues are thought by some scholars to have been personally sculpted by Maitani.

The Cathedral - Detail.

First Pilaster: The reliefs represent episodes from the creation of the world and of man according to the Book of Genesis. We see the creation of the animals, the story of Adam and Eve in Paradise, and after the Fall, the killing of Abel, and the invention of the Arts. A branch of ivy rising in the centre encircles and frames the separate stories arranged in six superimposed scenes.

Second Pilaster: *The messianic Prophecies. At the centre below we see Abraham sleeping. An acanthus plant – the Tree of Jesse – growing vertically, describes with its branches a series of ellipses in which David, Solomon, Rehoboam, Abijah, Asa, Jehoshophant, the Virgin Mary and Christ the Redeemer, are sculpted.*

Third Pilaster: Story of the New Testament. The scenes represented in ten reliefs are again divided by acanthus scrolls, within which we see (at the bottom) Adam sleeping, Angels in adoration, the Annunciation and Nativity, the Presentation in the Temple and the Flight into Egypt, the Massacre of the Innocents, the Crucifixion and the Noli me Tangere.

Fourth Pilaster: *Scenes of the Resurrection of the Flesh, the Last Judgement, Paradise and Hell are sculpted in five superimposed rows, and divided by vine branches. Particularly striking are the figures in the 4th and 5th row with the division of the Chosen from the Damned, the Resurrection of the Dead and the banishment of the Damned to Hell.*

THE FAÇADE AND THE ROSE WINDOW

Work on the construction of the magnificent façade of Orvieto Cathedral began around the year 1300, under the direction of Lorenzo Maitani, who had been called from his native Siena to accept the post of Master Builder of the Cathedral.

It was Maitani who substituted the façade's existing triple-gabled plan for the original single-gabled design usually attributed to Arnolfo di Cambio (who came from near Orvieto).

Divided into two superimposed orders, the façade is considered one of the glories of Gothic architecture in Italy.

The mosaics with which it is decorated have undergone various restorations and alterations in the course of the centuries.

Among the oldest of them are, however, those of the *"Baptism of Christ"* executed by Rossetti and Francesco Scalza after a cartoon by the local artist Cesare Nebbia.

The mosaic in the central gable on top, representing *"The Resurrection"* (again after a cartoon by Cesare Nebbia), was replaced in 1713 by a *"Coronation of the Virgin"* based on a painting by Lanfranco, but this has not survived and the existing mosaic of the same subject, dating to 1842, was in fact the work of a group of Roman mosaicists (including Cocchi and Castellini), based on a design by the Sienese Giovanni Bruno.

At the centre of the façade – below the mosaic of the "Coronation of the Virgin" – is the great rose window, the work of the Florentine artist Andrea di Cione, better known as Orcagna. This "precious gem", as it has justly been called, is formed of slender colonnettes and decorative elements of exquisite delicacy.

The head of the Redeemer is sculpted at its centre. Begun in 1354, the work was completed in 1380.

by Fra' Giovanni di Buccio Leonardelli, 1366.

L-M) St. Joachim and St. Anne, *by Iacopo of Bologna and Gabriele Mercanti, restored in 1713 and 1786.*

N) The nativity of Mary, *by Fra' Giovanni Leonardelli, 1364-1365.*

O) The Madonna with the Child, *a marble work attributed to Adrea Pisano – 1347.*

On the pillars there are the symbols of the four Evangelists.

P) The Angel, *symbol of St. Matthew;*

Q) The Lion, *symbol of St. Mark;*

R) The Eagle, *symbol of St. John;*

S) The Bull, *symbol of St. Luke.*

The bronze statues were made by Lorenzo Maitani (1329-1330).

On the top of the three lower spires:

T) St. Michael, *a bronze statue by Matteo Ugolino of Bologna* (1356).

U) Agnus dei (the Lamb of God), *a bronze work of the same artist.*

V) Angel, *a marble work of an unknown artists.*

On the upper spires, other marble statues of saints, made by various unknown artists of the 16th-17th century.

Z) In the centre of the upper wall of the facade, the beautiful rosewindow *by Andrea di Cione, called Orcagna.*

The four lower pillars of the facade.

1) The creation, and stories from Genesis.

2) The prophecies of the Redemption: continuation of the biblical storie.

3) Gospel stories.

4) The Last Judgement: Judgment, Paradise, Hell.

A SCHEME OF THE MOSAICS OF THE FAÇADE

A) Mary's wedding. *Remade in 1612 on designs of Antonio Pomarancio.*

B) The coronation of Mary. *Remade in 1842-1847, reproducing a fresco by Sano di Pietro existing in the «Palazzo Pubblico» of Siena.*

C) The presentation of Mary. *A work made in 1760-1763 on designs attributed to Giovanni Pomarancio.*

D-E) Gabriel and the Annunciation, *by Iacopo Pieruzzi 1649.*

F) The Baptism of Jesus, *on a design of Cesare Nebbia in 1584.*

G-H-I) The Assumption and the Apostles,

THE CENTRAL PORTAL AND THE BRONZE DOORS OF EMILIO GRECO

The large and imposing central door owes its grandeur to the two flat strips that circumscribe its splayed jambs, heightening all the richness and chiaroscuro of its mouldings. Traversing the façade from one side to the other, the horizontal cornice continues unbroken across the recessed bay in which the portal is set and provides the entablature below the bronze group, while the more slender string-course above it is interrupted to make way for the lunette, closed with sheets of alabaster, and housing a bronze canopy, its borders raised by six angels: the work is by Maitani. Under the canopy is the marble group of the Madonna and Child sculpted by Andrea Pisano in 1347. The modern bronze doors by the Sicilian sculptor Emilio Greco, without in any way detracting from the harmony of the façade, have replaced the old wooden doors of the Cathedral's three portals. The new doors were installed on 11 August 1970. In the central one, subdivided into 6 panels, are represented the seven works of Mercy: on the left, from top to bottom, «*Giving drink to the thirsty and food to the hungry*», «*Clothing the naked*», and «*Providing lodging for pilgrims*». On the right, again from top to bottom: «*Burying the dead*», «*Visiting the imprisoned*» and «*Visiting the sick*». The sides are sculpted with two large angels.

The central portal of the Cathedral and the new bronze doors.

Lunette of the central portal - Madonna and Child (Andrea Pisano XIV sec.)
The central portal.

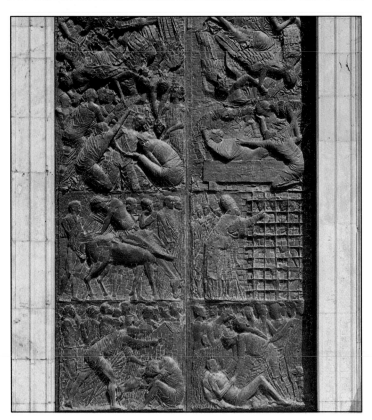

Visiting the sick.
Providing lodging for pilgrims.

Visiting the imprisoned.
Clothing the naked.

THE INTERIOR OF THE CATHEDRAL

Vast, simple and austere, the interior of the Cathedral combines the most precious elements of Lombard art. On entering this great basilica, the visitor is immediately struck by its spaciousness, the perspective effect of its massive columns, and its characteristic decoration in striped white and green marbles. The body of the church is divided into a nave, with lofty lean-to aisles and a clerestory of equally imposing dimensions; transepts; and a short square-ended choir. The series of columns carrying the round arches between the nave and its aisles are circular, tall and built up of dark and light stone in alternate regular courses. They are topped by elegant and richly foliated capitals, each of them different and eloquent demonstration of the innumerable figurative styles drawn on in Orvietan yards. The roofing of the Cathedral, installed by Maitani and finely decorated by Pietro di Lello and Vannuzzo di Mastro Pierino (1321-1330), was completely refurbished by Paolo Zampi and Paolo Cocchieri between 1881 and 1890. The aisles open out into a series of ten apsidal chapels, lit by narrow pointed windows, the lower half being filled with translucent alabaster, the upper with stained glass. In the transepts, respectively to the left and right of the choir, are the altars of the "Visitation of Mary" (by Simone Mosca, and Raffaello and Francesco da Montelupo) and the "Adoration of the Magi" (by Michele Sammicheli and Simone Mosca). In the right

The baptismal font.

transept is the Cappella Nuova (or Chapel of San Britius) with frescoes by Fra Angelico and Luca Signorelli (described below). Close to the entrance on the left is the *baptismal font*. It was begun by Luca di Giovanni in 1390, and completed in 1406, when the Sienese artist Sano di Matteo added the octagonal pyramid, surmounted by a statue of John the Baptist. Beside the baptismal font, on the left, a damaged *Madonna and Child* frescoed by Gentile di Fabriano (1425) is still visible. The figure of *Saint Catherine*, on the right of

the painting, a work by Giovambattista Ragazzini, was added in 1586. The frescoes in the apse are all of the Orvietan school. Painted by Ugolini di Prete Ilario and Pietro di Puccio (1370-1380), they were restored by Giacomo da Bologna in 1491 and later by Pinturicchio and Antonio da Viterbo (Il Pastura) in 1497. The frescoes – some of them partially destroyed – depict *episodes from the life of the Virgin*. The tall, narrow window at the east end (16. 30 m. high and 4. 55 m. broad) consists of 48 historiated oblong compartments depicting *scenes form the Life of*

Jesus and of the Virgin Mary; begun under Maitani's guidance in 1325, it was completed in 1334. The *Choir* was begun by the Sienese artist Giovanni Ammannati in 1329. Some scholars maintain that it too was designed by Maitani. The Cathedral's *monumental organ*, one of the biggest in Italy, was placed in the left transept, over the wall in which the entrance of the Cappella del Corporale is situated. The Magnificent organ-case was designed by the 16th century Orvietano artist Ippolito Scalza; the wooden ornaments were carved by Ercole Urbani and Gianni Carpentieri, while the instrument itself was produced by Bernardino

---

The Madonna with the Child (Gentile da Fabriano - 1425).

Apse - Stained-glass windows depicting episodes from the life of Christ and the Virgin.

Benvenuti. After undergoing various modifications in 1913, the organ was subjected to further work of maintenance and consolidation in 1975. The 4000 initial pipes have been increased to 5585 to permit the complete exploitation of its formidable musical resources.

The monumental organ.

THE GROUP OF THE PIETÀ

A work of the Orvietan painter, sculptor and architect Ippolito Scalza, this perfect group of four figures is sculpted from a single block of marble.

Scalza, it seems, began it in 1570 and worked on it for nine years. It is signed and dated 1579: «HIPPOLYTUS SCALZA URBEVETANUS MDLXXVIIII».

The work is remarkable for the exquisite finish of its rich draperies and the way in which the figures are conceived as a single group, united in spirit.

"Pietà" of Ippolito Scalza - 1579.

The Madonna of the Commended (Lippo Memmi - 1320).

THE CHAPEL OF THE CORPORAL

The left aisle leads, at the end of the transept, into the Chapel named after the Corporal (chalice-cloth) of the Miracle of Bolsena: the relic which is preserved in a reliquary over the principal altar. The walls of the Chapel are frescoed with episodes recounting the Miracle; dating to 1357-1363, they were probably executed by the Orvietan artists Ugolino di Prete Ilario, Domenico di Meo and Giovanni di Buccio Leonardelli. The vaults are painted with scenes from the Old and New Testament, while the other two walls are frescoed with scenes of miracles relating to the Sacrament of the Eucharist and a Crucifixion. The marble tabernacle, begun in 1358, bears the clear impress of Andrea Orcagna. The Chapel also contains, to the right, the painting known as the Madonna dei Raccomandati by the Sienese master Lippo Memmi.

RELIQUARY OF THE CORPORAL

It is the most important and precious work preserved in Orvieto Cathedral, and at the same time one of the greatest masterpieces of Sienese and Italian goldsmith's work. Com-missioned from the goldsmith Ugolino di Vieri by the Bishop of Orvieto, Beltramo Monalde-schi, in 1337, the reliquary was probably completed in Decem-ber 1339, the year in which the

Reliquary of the Corporal.

final payment for the work was made. The silver-gilt reliquary, resembling in form the façade of the Cathedral, is 1. 39 m. high and 0. 63 m. broad; it contains the sacred chalice-cloth of the Miracle of Bolsena. The surfaces of the reliquary are decorated with scenes in transparent enamel recounting episodes from the Miracle of Bolsena and the Life of Christ.

The open Reliquary, showing the Sacred Corporal, which is carried in procession on Corpus Christi and then remains on display in the Chapel.

THE CAPPELLA NUOVA OR CHAPEL OF THE MADONNA DI S. BRIZIO

The construction of the Cappella Nuova – later called the Chapel of the Madonna di San Brizio when the miraculous image of the Madonna of the same name was placed there – was decided by the Cathedral Board of Works in 1397.

The decoration of the Chapel, after lengthy negotiations with some of the leading artists of the time, including Perugino, was finally assigned to Luca Signorelli, who requested and obtained 575 ducats, of which one part in kind (wheat and wine), as well as a house. Signorelli began work on the Chapel's frescoes on 5 April 1499. His first task was to proceed to the completion of the two vaults begun a half century earlier by Fra Angelico and Benozzo Gozzoli.

Signorelli succeeded in recapturing the chromatic tones employed by his predecessors, while at the same time imbuing them with his own personality and art.

He worked on the Chapel's frescoes with great dedication for approximately two years; his mural paintings comprise representations of "The Doings of the Antichrist", "The Last Judgement", "The Resurrection of the Flesh", "The Damned", "The Blessed", "The Condemned descending into Hell" and "The Blessed ascending into Heaven".

The lower part of the Chapel's walls are decorated with arabesque and medallions of illustrious men, surrounded by scenes from ancient poetry. The theme originally chosen for the decoration of the Chapel – probably on the advice of some Orvietan theologians – was the Last Judgment, a recurrent one in 14th century Italian art. Signorelli's representation of the Last Judgment consists of a series of independent scenes, combined with "The Doings of the Antichrist", "The Prophecies" and "The Destruction of the World".

DOINGS OF THE ANTICHRIST

On entering the Cappella Nuova, on the wall to the left, we see the Doings of the Antichrist, which Signorelli has depicted with great scenic sense and narrative skill.

At the centre of the fresco, in the forefront, we see the Antichrist addressing the people from on top of a pedestal.

He is being prompted by a devil at his shoulder.

To the left, the followers of the Antichrist kill several Christians, while the scene of the end of the Antichrist is depicted above.

The elaborate temple in the background is thought to symbolise Jerusalem.

Doings of the antichrist (detail).
Self portrait of Luca Signorelli (on the left), standing next to Fra Angelico.
The decorations of the Cappella Nuova are Signorelli's greatest masterpiece.

HELL

Before beginning his representation of Hell, Signorelli must undoubtedly have studied the bas-reliefs of the fourth pilaster of the façade. But in carrying out the work he preferred to play down the descriptive element and epitomise the desperation of the damned in a single scene. The devils launch themselves on the terrified crowd of the damned, conscious of the inexorable punishments that await them. A furious struggle breaks out: the damned try in vain to shake off their persecutors. One devil, at the centre of the fresco, is carrying a woman on his shoulder, while others hurl the bodies of two damned on to the seething mass below. Three angels – above to the right – are shown drawing their swords and standing in guard over the terrible scene.

The Damned in Hell – (Detail) – Due to the dramatic force which Signorelli's brush has given to these images of torment, a true visual interpretation of Dante's description of Hell, this fresco is considered the finest in the Chapel. At the centre: The Whore of Babylon, being carried away by a devil. According to a popular tradition, Signorelli modelled the Whore of Babylon on a woman from Orvieto who had accepted his advances, but later rejected him.

THE CROWNING OF THE ELECT

The refined and delicate beauty of the scene, the harmonious elegance of the bodies – not by chance has Signorelli depicted them nude – and the ineffable sweetness of the faces of the Elect, patiently awaiting the call to Heaven, are expressive both of the sublimity of the moment and their gratitude to the Almighty.

In the highly expressive faces of the Elect Signorelli has managed to convey their joy at having been granted the coveted prize. The importance he has given to the scene of the Elect, who all conform to a single type of refined and delicate beauty, contrasts with that given to the Angels, who seem more variegated, more individually characterized, more humanized. The effect was intentional on Signorelli's part: the impact of the scene derives from just this contrast in forms and expressions.

THE ANGELS LEADING THE ELECT TO HEAVEN AND THE ENTRANCE TO HELL

These frescoes over the windows represent a pictorial version of Dante's account of the Entrance to Hell and the Angels leading the Elect to Heaven. Signorelli has depicted the Reprobates at the foot of two large mountains, along the banks of Acheron, where we see a devil with a white banner leading away a group of the damned: the slothful. Other damned give way to despair and lamentation because they see Charon approaching in his boat. Below, Minos is intent on inflicting punishment on a reprobate. Above, two angels, one dressed in armour and the other in veils, stand guard over the scene. On the other side (photograph to the left), a group of nine angels playing musical instruments show the Blessed the way to Heaven.

THE FRESCOES OF THE VAULTS

The decorations of the Chapel vaulting, left unfinished by Fra Angelico in 1447, were completed by Signorelli 52 years later. Fra Angelico only managed to complete two panels of the vaulting above the altar representing the *"Chorus of Prophets"* and *"Christ as Judge"*.

Signorelli finished the painting of the ceiling with *"Angels and the emblems of the Passion"*, *"The Apostles"*, *"The Doctors"*, *"The Masters"*, *"The Virgin"* and *"The Prophets"*.

The Calling of the Elect to Heaven - (Detail).

The Calling of the Elect to Heaven
Two angels at the centre scatter roses over the virtuous, while above, seated on clouds, a further nine angels call the Elect with their music. The delicate sequence of colours give a wonderful sense of harmony to the whole picture.

THE RESURRECTION OF THE FLESH

On the wall opposite that on which Signorelli has depicted the Doings of the Antichrist, the Resurrection of the Flesh echoes – albeit with some slight variation – the theme and serene, poetically suggestive "atmosphere" of the call of the Elect.

In this scene the master has deliberately avoided the traditional iconographic conventions of the subject: instead of the usual tombs flung open under the pressure of the resurrected bodies beneath, he has set his pictorial narrative on a plane completely devoid of any other figurative element, presumably so as to give his fresco greater emotional and scenic force. The bodies of the Risen – in all the fullness of their physical vigour – reemerge, albeit laboriously, from the soil, take their first steps, embrace each other tenderly, or lift their faces and arms up to heaven. They have risen with new and youthful bodies invested with reacquired innocence.

Two large Angels on high blow elongated horns to wake the dead. At this point of the fresco, an underlying preparatory drawing of eight nude figures sketched in bare outline by Signorelli was disclosed by the restorations in 1940.

A *detail of the* Resurrection of the Flesh.

THE DESTRUCTION OF THE WORLD

This fresco occupies the great arch above the entrance to the Chapel. The restricted semicircular space did not prevent Signorelli from expressing all his talent and the grandeur of his creative genius.

The composition, which has nothing ornamental about it, is distributed with the greatest skill and in full respect for the material restraints of the space and the narrative requirements of the subject. The human figures – very large below but gradually diminishing in size – give great perspective force to the scene. To the right of the fresco we see the Sybil's heralding of the cataclysm; David, portrayed together with the prophets Enoch and Elijah, indicates the stars being obscured. Fire rains down from the sun, while a couple flee from the rubble of a temple destroyed by an earthquake and are received by a group of old people. Above, three youths are stripped and tortured. The ruins of a devastated city and the wreckage of ships are driven by a tidal wave towards the hills.

On top, four angels hurl themselves on humanity; people flee from the approaching flames. Some mothers clasp their children to their breast in the attempt to protect them. In the foreground, seven soldiers in magnificent multi-coloured hose.

The flight of men and women faced by the end of the world. Figures of soldiers in the foreground - some of whom are lying on the ground - in their brightly - coloured mail, are taken by surprise by the cataclysm.

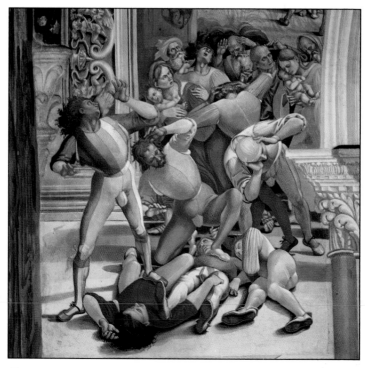

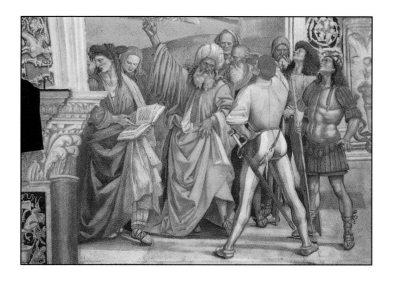

The noble figure of David stands at the centre of the scene, between the Sibyl, who is predicting the end of the world, and the prophets.

THE MAIN FRESCOES OF THE CHAPEL

The main frescoes of the Chapel are accompanied below by a decorative wainscotting in which Signorelli – presumably to give further clarification to their iconographic programme – has portrayed, within large medallions, some famous poets and scenes from their works.

The series begins below the fresco of the Antichrist with a portrait of Homer and three episodes from the Iliad.

Below the fresco of the Destruction of the World the Greek philosopher Empedocles is shown bending over bakwards; he seems to be leaning out from the wall as he looks up at the scenes of his prophecy.

The series of the poets is continued under the fresco of the Resurrection, where Lucan is portrayed together with two scenes from the "Pharsalia": the Massacre of the Pompeians and the Killing of Pompey.

The portrait of Horace is surrounded by four medallions in which scenes from the Odes are depicted.

Ovid, in the following medallion, seems to be turning to address an invisible interlocutor; the four accompanying scenes represent episodes from the "Metamorphoses".

Virgil, in turn, seems visibly distressed as he looks back at the fresco of the Damned above him.

Dante, accompanied by scenes from the first two cantos of the "Purgatory", is shown at work.

A further two medallions represent The martyrdom of St. Faustino and the killing of St. Pietro Parenzo by Orvietan heretics (1199).

43

THE PALAZZO SOLIANO (OR PALAZZO DEI PAPI)
THE CATHEDRAL MUSEUM (OPERA DEL DUOMO)

The Papal Palace (the Palazzo dei Papi), also known as the Palazzo Soliano, after the name of the district in which it is situated, stands to the right of the Cathedral. This handsome and monumental building in the Gothic style was probably begun by Urban IV during his brief pontificate (1261-1264), and continued by Martin IV between 1281 and 1285. With the transfer of the papacy to Avignon in 1309, the building – i. e. the part to the rear of the existing complex – remained unfinished. Under Boniface VIII (Benedetto Caetano of Anagni, Pope from 1294 to 1303), its frontal extension was added in c. 1297; it consists of spacious superimposed halls, the upper one accessible by a monumental external staircase. This latter was certainly intended to house Consistories and Councils, since the Pope and his court often sought refuge in Orvieto during this period. In 1550 the building was sold by the Commune of Orvieto to the Cathedral's Board of Works and restored in 1896 by the architect Paolo Zampi, who added its upper windows and crenellation. Today, the Cathedral Museum (the Museo dell'Opera del Duomo) is housed in the front wing of the building. At the centre of the large hall on the first floor' panels from a polyptych by Simone Martini (1280-1344) can be admired;

General view of the main hall of the Museum.

they represent the Madonna and Child, Saints Peter and Paul, and Saints Mary Magdalen and Dominic. The Museum also contains some splendid examples of medieval goldsmith's work, notably the reliquary of the skull of Saint Savino (1340), a masterpiece by the Sienese goldsmiths Ugolino di Vieri and Viva di Lando. Various frescoes removed from churches in Orvieto are displayed on the entrance wall. Against the other walls are fragments of the roof and tie beams from the Cathedral, a Madonna and Child with Saints Savino and Giovenale, a tile frescoed with a self-portrait of Signorelli and a portrait of Nicola di Angelo Franchi, chamberlain of the Cathedral's Board of Works in 1500. The Museum also houses the designs on parchment for the façade of the Cathedral: one with only a single gable, attributed by some to Arnolfo di Cambio and by others to Maitani; the other triple-gabled and universally assigned to Maitani. Facing the façade of the Cathedral is the Palazzo dell'Opera del Duomo (Cathedral Board of Works). Built in 1359, it was enlarged and altered by the architect Vespignani in 1857 and later by Paolo Zampi. The building contains the Cathedral's administrative offices and archives. The first floor houses a magnificent collection of Etruscan, Corinthian and Greek vases, and other interesting finds from Etruscan tombs in the environs of Orvieto.

EMILIO GRECO MUSEUM

The Emilio Greco Museum is installed on the ground-floor of the Palazzo Soliano. The broad and elegant nave houses the collection of sculptural and graphic works donated by Emilio Greco, one of the greatest Italian sculptors of our time, to the city of Orvieto, to which he was artistically linked because he had sculpted the majestic bronze portals of the nearby Duomo during the Sixties. The 32 sculptures, for the most part in bronze, and the 60 graphic works, including original drawings, lithographs and etchings, cover the main stages in Greco's artistic career. They range from *the* Wrestler, a bronze of 1947, and the Portrait of a Lady, a small ink drawing of 1946, to the artist's last works in the Eighties, such as: the Dormitio Virginis, a bronze bas-relief of 1983, and the copper etching Amorous Composition 1989. Among other things, the museum houses the original plaster model, over six metres high, of the monument to Pope John XXIII, the bronze version of which is in St. Peter's. The display of the works, designed by the architect Giulio Savio, is arranged along a system of walkways placed at different levels, which divide the space and enable the works to be viewed from unusual perspectives. The Museum was conceived in conformity with the most up-to-date criteria of Museum display. A high-tech system was in fact adopted to ensure the optimum protection of the environment and conservation of the works. Particular attention was devoted to the provision of special facilities to permit visit to the museum by the handicapped. A multi-media space permits the organization of cultural and educational activities. Lastly, sales-points and a bookshop offer the public a range of products connected with the museum's exhibitional and cultural activities.

Emilio Greco Museum - Interior.

THE "CLAUDIO FAINA" ARCHAEOLOGICAL MUSEUM

The Palazzo Faina, which houses the "Claudio Faina" Museum, is situated on the opposite side of the Piazza del Duomo, facing the Cathedral façade. The Museum, which is the property of the municipality of Orvieto but is run by the Faina Foundatio, began as the private collection amassed by Count Mauro Faina in Perugia in the 1860s.

Later transferred to Orvieto, it was considerably enlarged with finds made in the area. The great floor contains a fine collection of archaeological remains, including objects found within the town of Orvieto itself and others recovered from the Croce del Tufo necropolis.

Objects of particular interest include a *tomb-stone* from Croce del Tufo, a cinerary urn, the so-called *Venus* of Cannicella, and the *polychrome sarcophagus* found in the nearby village of Torre San Severo in 1912: finds which date from the 6th to the 2nd centuries B. C.

Memorial stones with Etruscan inscriptions and cremation urns of the Villanovan period are displayed on the first floor.

Particularly fine is the collection of Etruscan *bucchero* (black pottery) dating to the 6th and 5th century B.C., vases, drinking cups, weapons and armour. The Museum also contains numerous Black- and Red-figure vases imported from Greece and dating from 560 to 530 B. C.

Apart from three large amphorae signed by EXEKIAS (second half of the 6th century B. C.), displayed in the central display-case, there are also a series of Etruscan Red-figure vases, another series of silvered vases and a third of small Etruscan can a Roman statues.

Of the many other finds on display, the three Orvietan vases are distinguished by their stylistic details and unusual decoration.

The "Claudio Faina" Archaeological Museum - Interior.

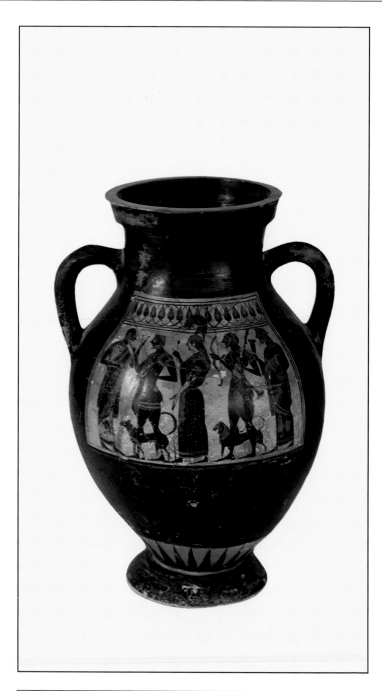

Black-Figure Attic Amphora by the "Amasis Painter" (550 B. C.).
Provenance: Vulci (?). Valentini Bonaparte Collection.

Right: Etruscan art – Peperino sarcophagus. (3th century B. C.). Below: Black-Figure Attic Amphora by Exekias (540 B. C.). Provenance: Orvieto – Croce del Tufo Necropolis.

49

NECROPOLIS OF TUFA CRUCIFIX

A considerable part of the rocky mass on which Orvieto stands, and of the surrounding countryside, is characterized by the presence of numerous necropoleis, the so-called "cities of the dead". These are an important witness to Etruscan civilisation. The most important tombs from the historical and artistic viewpoint are those concentrated around the Necropolis of the Tufa Crucufix (8th to 3rd centuries B.C.). Other tombs are scattered around the whole area. The most famous are the so-called Settecamini (Seven Chimneys), inside which were found funerary objects and paintings which are now kept in the city museums or in those of Florence. The frescoes, carefully removed from the walls of the tombs, can now be admired in the new archaeological exhibition room on the ground floor of the palace of the Popes. They have been placed in Etruscan tombs reconstructed in their actual dimensions. The tombs of the Cannicella, situated on the southern side of the tufa mass, cannot be visited, since they have been covered with surface detritus, washed down in recent decades. As mentioned above, the most interesting area of the tombs is the one known as the necropolis of the Tufa Crucifix. This is on the state road between the railway station of Orvieto Scalo and the town. It is clearly signposted, and there is ample space in a car-park from which a short lane leads to the necropolis. The series of chamber-tombs is arranged in such away that it forms a real city of the dead, since they are distributed along a road and gathered and organised in groups as if they were lit-

Partial view of Necropolis.

tle inhabited centres. The blocks of tufa which abound in the area were used to build them. The large throne placed before the entrance is of great interest, as is the inscription carrying the name of the defunct, which is carved over the architrave of the door. The important funerary objects and all the utensils which were brought to light are on display in the Faina Museum. It should be noted that like the whole outcrop of Orvieto, this area is honeycombed with tunnels and underground passages which were used from the Etruscan period onwards. From the necropolis, the former church of Sant'Agostino can be seen perched on the edge of the rocky precipice, and also one of the most ancient religious buildings in Orvieto, the church of San Giovenale.

THE CHURCHES OF ORVIETO

According to the historian Pericle Perali, the rock on which Orvieto stands already constituted the site of a city in Etruscan times, and one that differed from the other Etruscan cities by virtue of its importance as a religious centre. This assumption is reinforced by the numerous Etruscan tombs found in its immediate vicinity, by the existence of a number of areas on which temples once stood. Again, in Perali's view, Orvieto occupies the site of the famed "Fanum Voltumnae", the sanctuary in which the twelve peoples of Etruria held their most important politico-religious meetings.

How long the tufa rock on which Orvieto stands remained deserted after the destruction of "Fanum Voltumnae" cannot be determined with any precision. Yet already by the 1st century A. D. it had been newly inhabited and Roman temples had risen over the ruins of their Etruscan predecessor.

These were, in turn, to be transformed into churches. The site of the ancient Etruscan forum was also occupied by the Roman forum and the basilica, which were later to become the Piazza del Comune and the Church of Saint'Andrea.

But little remains of the city's temples other than a few fragmentary remains such as the Roman floor of the church of Sant'Andrea and the many Etruscan remains visible in its crypt.

There are many churches in Orvieto which are worth visiting on account of their ancient origins, their artistic splendour and the works of art they preserve.

The Cathedral, that authentic jewel of Italian Gothic art, we have already described. The most important of the other churches are summarily described below.

Apart from these, other churches of lesser importance, but of no less interest for their antiquity or artistic qualities, are well worth visiting.

In the Via Ghibellina is the **Church of the Gesù**, dating to 1618, with an interior notable for its splendid baroque stuccowork. Over the high altar is the Madonna known as the "morto vivo" (meaning someone dead being brought back to life): a name it derived from the fact that Cardinal Simoncelli invoked it while lying at death's door, and was granted a recovery.

In the Piazza de' Ranieri is the baroque **church of San Lodovico**, which contains, among other works, a tempera painting on canvas, probably a gonfalon or banner, over the altar to the left; painted by Andrea di Giovanni (1410), it represents "The Innocents adoring the Child Jesus in the Glory of Paradise", and is notable for the rarity of its subject-matter and the ingenuous charm of its figura style.

In the Piazza del Popolo, facing the Palazzo del Capitano, is the Romanesque **church of San Rocco**, with the remains of fresco decorations: in the apse, Christ between the Virgin, the Baptist, St. Roche and St. Sebastian, a work by Cristoforo da Marsciano (1527), and a Madonna and Child with 4 Saints painted by Eusebio da Montefiascone.

The church of the **Santi Apostoli** have an elegant belfry, but its façade has has remained unfinished.

THE CHURCH OF SAN GIOVENALE

By taking the picturesque road skirting the rock-face from the Porta Maggiore, or starting out from the Piazza della Repubblica by the Via Filippeschi, and then going down the Via Malabranca, we reach the Church of San Giovenale.

Pre-Romanesque in origin, it was commissioned by seven nobles of Orvieto, including the Counts of Marsciano and the Monaldeschi, and built over the ruins of a previous building in 1004.

Considerably altered in its original structure (shorn of its ancient apse, demolished when the church was prolonged to the east in the Gothic period), its interior consists of a nave and two aisles divided by eight cylindrical columns in tufa supporting round arches.

The Church of San Giovenale.

The Church of San Giovenale - Interior.

The transepts are Gothic and date from the church's enlargement in the mid-13th century. The surviving frescoes on the walls (others have been lost) are of the Orvietan school of the 13th and 16th centuries: the most important represent the *Annunciation*, the *Nativity*, and the *Madonna with St. Sebastian*.

The high altar dates from 1170 with an altar-frontal in the Byzantine style carved with interlaced ornament, figures of bishops and priests and symbolic signs.

The simple façade has a door with a round arch; to its left stands the ponderous bell-tower, its upper storey rebuilt in the 17th century.

The travertine portal admitting into the right aisle of the church was opened in 1497; it is surmounted by a lunette containing a bust of St. Giovenale.

The head of St. Savino is venerated in this church; the two saints – Giovenale and Savino – were, it seems, the first to bring Christianity to Orvieto.

Close to San Giovenale is the former church of **Sant'Agostino** dating to the 13th century, with an elegant Gothic portal (1445). The church belonged to the Augustinians and the conventual Franciscans.

THE CHURCH OF SAN LORENZO DE' ARARI

Since the former church was too close to the monastery of San Francesco and the pealing of its bells disturbed the Friars Minor, the latter requested that it be demolished and rebuilt "forty poles further away".

Their wish was granted, with the proviso that the new church (1292) be an exact copy of the old. Disfigured during the baroque period, the church was later restored by the architect Paolo Zampi. It has an extremely simple façade with an unassuming 15th-century portal in the lunette of which, – much deteriorated – is an image of the *Madonna and Child with two Saints*.

Above the portal, almost at the apex of the façade, is a little rose-window. The church has a small belfry with single and twin-arched windows and a semi-circular apse.

The interior, of basilica type, has a nave and two aisles divided by ten hefty Romanesque columns with round arches which support the heavy walls. At the end of the nave, to the left, are frescoes dating to 1330, and recently restored, of the "*Life and Martyrdom of St. Laurence*".

Other paintings, rather damaged, may be seen elsewhere in the church, such as that of *St. Laurence, St. Bridget* and *St. William Abbot* on the first column to the left; or that of *St. Nicholas* and another bishop saint on another column.

In the main chapel is an altar with a 12th-century *ciborium* similar to that of the Miracle of Bolsena. The top of the altar rests on a cippus found beneath the church, which probably occupies the site of an Etruscan shrine. Over the altar is a small 14th century *Crucifix*.

In the apse are preserved some 14th century frescoes in the Byzantine manner with "*Christ enthroned*" and *Saints Laurence, Mary, John* and *Francis*.

THE CHURCH OF SAN GIOVANNI

Going down the ancient Via Ranieri, we turn to the left along the Via Ripa di Serancia and, come to the piazza in which the Church of San Giovanni Evangelista stands.

It has a simple 16th century façade and a characteristic octagonal interior. To the left of the entrance is an elegant 15th century ciborium, while various medieval epigraphic and architectural fragments of the 10th-13th centuries are built into the walls. In the apse is a 14th century painting of the *Madonna and Child*, known as the Madonna della Fonte (Madonna of the Spring).

The church, which was originally the priory of the Hermits of St. Augustine and later (in 1498) Abbey of the Lateran Canons, is reputed to have been built at the behest of Pope John X in 916. In the adjoining monastery, which now serves as a venue for exhibitions and conferences, there is a beautiful cloister, whose design has been attributed to Sangallo; at its centre is an elegant marble well- head dating to 1526-32.

The Church of San Giovanni.

THE CHURCH OF SAN FRANCESCO

Not far from the Church of San Lorenzo de Arari, by taking the Via Filippo Scalza, we reach the Piazza Febbei in which the Church of San Francesco is located. Built in the Gothic style at the expense of the Republic and nobility of Orvieto in 1230, it was inaugurated and consecrated by Clement IV. Enlarged by St. Bonaventura, it was completely remodelled in the 18th century. But it still retains its simple Gothic façade (1240), from which three Gothic portals lead into the interior. The central one of these is of unusual elegance and ornateness, with splayed jambs, rich mouldings and marble twisted colonnettes. The architrave is surmounted by the sign of the *lamb*, the emblem of the Chapter that contributed to the cost of the church's construction. The interior consists of a single nave with intecommunicating chapels in a sober baroque style. The wooden Crucifix, attributed to Maitani, is of exceptional beauty. Also of considerable artistic value is the painting by Cesare Nebbia over the high altar. The church is no less notable for the important historical events that took place in it. It was here, in 1273, that Gregory X celebrated the funeral of Henry of England, nephew of King Henry III, who had been stabbed to death in the church of San Silvestro in Viterbo by Guy de Montfort in revenge for the death of his father Simon de Montefort (leader of the barons' revolt against Henry III) at the battle of Evesham (1265). It was here, too, that Boniface VIII canonized Louis IX King of France on 11 August 1267, and that the architect Ippolito Scalza was buried.

A Franciscan monastery formerly existed next to the church; it later became a Jesuit college. It now houses a school and is also used as an exhibition centre. The monastic complex still retains its elegant arcaded cloister, designed by Ippolito Scalza, at the centre of which is a handsome well-head installed by St. Bonaventura.

THE CHURCH OF SANTA MARIA DEI SERVI

The church is situated close to the Piazza Cahen, in an attractive little piazza on the Corso Cavour. Originally Gothic, it was built in 1265 and acquired by the Servants of Mary friars from the Abbot and Monks of San Severo in 1265.

On falling into ruins, the church was completely reconstructed in a chaste neo-classic style by the architect Virginio Vespignani in 1857.

The interior consists of a single nave and contains a beautiful *holy water stoup* dating to 1497; the work of Antonio Federighi, it bears the arms of the Borgia family.

Other notable works of art in the church include a wooden 14th century *Crucifix*, some 16th century frescoes and – of exceptional interest – a panel painting of the *Madonna and Child with Angels* situated to the right of the high altar. This latter is a work by the Florentine painter Coppo di Marcovaldo (1265-70), and has temporarily been removed for restoration; while awaiting its return, we publish a reproduction of the panel prior to restoration.

Other paintings preserved in the church include: "*St. Sebastian*" by Vincenzo Pontani", "*St. Martin*" by Raffaele Puccetti, and some recently restored 16th century frescoes contained in a little chapel.

The Church of Santa Maria dei Servi.

THE CHURCH OF SAN DOMENICO

Situated in the Piazza XXIX Marzo, the church may be reached either by the Via Belisario or from the Piazzale Cahen in a few minutes walk.

It was founded in 1233-64, perhaps over the ruins of a putative Temple of Minerva. According to tradition, it was the first church to be dedicated to St. Dominic. Gothic in style, as shown by the handsome portal set in its simple façade, it was originally 90 m. long and divided into a nave and two aisles. But it was completely transformed in the course of the centuries and eventually reduced to its apse and transept alone, remodelled in the baroque style.

The adjacent monastery of San Domenico has also unfortunately disappeared: it was completely demolished in 1934 to make way for the women's Academy of Physical Education, now the Military School of Physical Education.

St. Thomas Aquinas stayed in this monastery for several year. Despite its reduction, the church still contains some notable works of art in its interior, such as a beautiful 14th century wooden *Crucifix* attributed to a follower of Giovanni Pisano.

The body of the Blessed Vanna da Carnaiola, who died in Orvieto in 1306, is preserved in an urn below one of the altars.

From one of the chapels flanking the sanctuary steps lead down to the underground *"Petrucci Chapel"* (1517); its noble Doric architecture designed by Sanmicheli da Verona, it is oc-

tagonal in plan and was formerly decorated with marbles, metals and polychrome majolicas, now sadly deteriorated.

The church also preserves a number of paintings of the Umbrian school of the 14-15th centuries, such as the fresco of "*Crucifixion with the Virgin and St. John*" visible in the first chapel to the right.

The most important work preserved in San Domenico is, however, the *funerary monument of the French Cardinal De Braye.*

This is a major work by the great sculptor from Colle Val d'Elsa, Arnolfo di Cambio; dating to 1282, it is exceptionally signed by him. Situated to the left of the entrance, the tomb, though clumsily recomposed after having been transferred from its original position, remains a jewel of 13th century Italian art.

The central part of the monument, over the sarcophagus, represents the dead *Cardinal* recumbent on a bed with two angels drawing back the curtains of a canopy.

Above is the statue of the *Madonna and Child*: at her feet, to the left, the Cardinal being presented to the Virgin; to the right, St. Dominic.

Other dismembered fragments from the tomb, such as two headless angels with censer, are now preserved in the Cathedral Museum.

To the left of the altar, in a case, is the *chair of St. Thomas Aquinas*, who taught theology in the adjoining Dominican monastery for several years; in Orvieto at the time of the Miracle of Bolsena (1263), he composed there the Office of Corpus Christi at the behest of Pope Urban IV.

THE CHURCH OF SANT'ANDREA

According to the well-known historian Pericle Perali, the church was founded in the 6th century over the ruins of an Etruscan temple in the area of the ancient Forum, as would seem to be testified by the Etruscan remains visible in its crypt. Rebuilt in the 11-12th century, and completed in the 14th, the church is unusual in construction.

Its façade, graced by an upper rose-window and a 15th century Gothic portal, is flanked, to the right, by a massive dodecagonal, crenellated bell-tower, with coats-of-arms walled into its lower storeys and three storeys of mullioned windows above. The tower resembles the belfry of the Abbey of Saints Severo and Martirio outside Orvieto.

Flanking the left side of the church is a portico, demolished in 1213, but reconstructed in 1926.

Under the portico, whose arcades are supported by travertine co-

lumns with emblems of the six major guilds, a large Latin inscription embellished with coats-of-arms commemorates the glorious past of the church, which served, in the Middle Ages, as the seat of the flourishing Commune. In fact, meetings of citizens were held, and decisions taken, inside the church at the time of the medieval republic of Orvieto. It was here, too, that Innocent III proclaimed the 4th Crusade in 1216; that Pope Honorius III crowned Pierre d'Artois King of Jerusalem in 1217; that the Podestà of Orvieto Pietro Parenzo, killed by the Patarini in 1199, was canonized in the same year; that the future popes Nicholas IV and Boniface VIII were raised to the Cardinalate in the presence of Charles of Anjou in 1281; and that the general council of Orvieto decided in 1338 to bear the statue of the Madonna Assunta in procession to the Cathedral on

The Church of Sant'Andrea.

the eve of the feast of the Assumption (15 August) to implore her help in liberating Orvieto from the prolonged siege to which she had been subjected: a procession which is still repeated with great soleminity today.

The interior of Sant'Andrea is of basilica type with a nave and two aisles divided by monolithic columns of oriental granite with capitals of classical type, and a double transept.

As Fumi points out in his monograph on Orvieto, it displays some analogy with the architectural forms of the interior of the Cathedral.

At the beginning of the right aisle, a wrought-iron gate gives access to the crypt, where recent excavations have uncovered the foundations of the ancient 6th century basilica with impressive remains of its geometric mosaic floor and, at an even deeper level, remains dating to the Etruscan period.

In view of the central role it has played in the public life of Orvieto, and the historic events enacted within it, the church of Sant'Andrea is one of the most important religious buildings in the town.

THE ABBEY OF SAINTS SEVERO AND MARTIRIO

According to an ancient legend, when St. Severo, a monk of the Intocrina valley in the territory of Antrodoco, died at the end of the 6th century, his remains were taken to Orvieto in a cart drawn by two "untamed bullocks".

Rotunda, a noble lady, followed by the people, went to meet the cart in order to take possession of the Saint's body, but her hand remained attached to the coffin and she only succeeded in loosening her grip once she had solemnly sworn to donate the chapel of San Silvestro and a large part of her estate which surrounded it as the last resting-place of the Saint.

But historically, the ancient origins of the Abbey are shrouded in the mists of time, though it is presumed that it was begun in the 6th century.

It was reconstructed by the Benedictines in the 12th century, but they were expelled from the Abbey in 1220 for rebelling against the authority of the bishop.

Subsequently it was given to the French order of Premonstratensian Canons, who enlarged it by building a large refectory, a cloister – now destroyed – and a chapter house in a mixed Romanesque- Gothic style.

The Abbey of Saint Severo and Martirio – or "The Badia" as it is now commonly known – is built on the slopes of a hill looking

The Abbey of Saints Severo and Martirio.

towards Orvieto (about 4 km. away) and within easy reach of the Autostrada del Sole.

On arriving at the abbey complex, we see to the right the *Church of the Crucifix* and the ancient *refectory* with frescoes of the 12th-14th century. To the left are the ruins of the *Chapter House*. In one part, it still retains its Gothic vaulting, in which an arch frames a picturesque panoramic view of Orvieto's rock outcrop with the town, and especially the Cathedral, rising over it.

We then enter a courtyard planted with trees, where the Abbey's guest-house in Romanesque-Gothic style is situated; this has now been converted into a restaurant and first-class hotel.

To the left is the *ancient church*, with a fine Gothic portal.

The interior consists of a single nave roofed by a ribbed vault.

The Cosmatesque floor is still, in part, in an excellent state of preservation.

The high altar (1100) is supported by two Roman bas-reliefs. Particularly beautiful is the church's crenellated *bell-tower*.

Dodecagonal in shape, it has two upper storeys of twin-arched and single-arched windows.

Its bell (nicknamed "viola") is renowned for its delicate sound.

THE POZZO DI SAN PATRIZIO

From the Piazza Cahen – between the Fortezza dell'Albornoz, the former funicular station and the gardens surrounding the remains of an Etruscan temple – a short tree-lined avenue leads down to the panoramic terrace where one of Orvieto's main attractions is located: the Pozzo di San Patrizio or St. Patrick's Well.

The well was sunk by Pope Clement VII (the Florentine Giulio de' Medici) during his stay in Orvieto where he had sought refuge during the Sack of Rome in December 1527. The Florentine architect Antonio da Sangallo the Younger was commissioned to carry out the work. After a suitable source of water had been located in the *Fonti di San Zero* at the foot of the rock (the immediate environs of Orvieto were once prolific in natural springs), the work was immediately begun and, during Sangallo's absences, continued under the direction of Giovan Battista da Cortona.

In 1532, at a depth of 200 feet, a pre-Etruscan tomb was discovered. After the tufa seam had been dug through, the work of excavation continued through successive strata of tertiary clay, while the central shaft and well shafts were built out of tufa blocks and bricks. The well was not finished until 1537 under the pontificate of Paul III (Alessandro Farnese).

This artesian well - a formidable piece of engineering - was sunk to

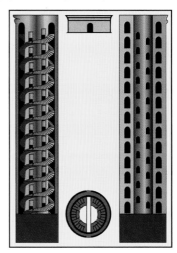

ensure water supplies in the event of the town being besieged. Another version about the method used in its construction has it that the excavations began from the bottom, first by digging a short lateral shaft into the rock and then continuing upwards; the excavated material would then have fallen by its own gravity and could have been removed with greater simplicity.

The well, which is circular in section, is approximately 62 metres deep and 13. 40 metres wide. Two diametrically opposite doors lead into two concentric spiral staircases, the one superimposed over the other, in such a way as to be independent of each other and non-communicating; thus preventing those coming up from obstucting those going down. Lit by 70 windows, each stairway consists of 248 comfortable steps, almost like a ramp, and easy to descend even for pack animals which went down to drink at the well from a wooden bridge, just above the water level, where the stairway ended, before going back up the opposite stairway. The descent of the well is a fascinating experience, both in view of its unique method of construction and the sensations it arouses: the temperature drops gradually as one descends, and the light grows less and less, and it appears splashed with patches of blue and pale green, from the vegetation which in part covers the walls.

The well, which has been visited with extraordinary curiosity ever since it was first opened in 1556, later came to be known as the "Pozzo di San Patrizio", because it was thought to resemble, albeit vaguely, the chasm which plummeted down from the Irish cave in which St. Patrick used to withdraw to pray.

An elegant Latin inscription, carved on two plaques attached to the two entrances, epitomises the reasons why this artesian well was built: : «Quod Natura Munimento Inviderat Industria Adiecit».

The Pozzo di San Patrizio and interior.

THE WALLS AND GATES OF THE TOWN

According to the historian of Orvieto Pericle Perali, the typography of the town in the Etruscan period cannot be determined with any certainty. Certainly, however, access to it was provided by a single approach, hewn out of the tufa rock: the gate corresponding to the present Porta Maggiore. From this point, on the western side of the town, the ancient "decumanus" – or principal East-West throughfare – perhaps started out, intersecting the "cardo" – or North-South street – in what is now the Piazza della Repubblica.

It was here, again in Perali's view, that the greatest and holiest of the Etruscan temples, the one dedicated to Voltumna, was situated.

The "decumanus" – its first stretch known in the Middle Ages, as now, as the Via della Cava, a name alluding to the artificial origin of its opening *cava* – meaning quarry in Italian – led (along what is now the Corso Cavour) to the eastern end of the town, where another entrance was later opened. This was the "Porta Soliana". Its primitive form is no longer visible, since it was built over in the Middle Ages and turned into a secret postern (the

Porta Maggiore.

Porta Postierla). Later still, it changed into the Porta Rocca following its incorporation in the defences of the fortress built above it between 1364 and 1456: the Fortezza dell'Albornoz. Another ancient gate was the Porta di Santa Maria close to the Duomo; later blocked up, it was reopened in the 14th century, but finally abandoned in the 16th. On the northern side of the rock was yet another gate known as the Porta Vivaria (or Scenditoio). In the 12th century a new gate was opened to the west of the Surripa district. This was the Porta Pertusa, which was replaced by the present Porta Romana in 1822. Later, in 1833, the Porta Cassia was built between the Porta Vivaria and Porta Postierla, while to the east access to the town was facilitated by the water-powered funicular installed (by the engineer Bracci) in 1888; this entered the town through a tunnel dug through the rock and provided a direct approach from the railway station below. In the 13th and 14th century the gates were guarded by special custodians periodically elected by the Commune. Of the walls of Orvieto little can be said. The tufa rock itself, with its sheer cliffs varying in height from twenty to thirty metres, provided, in effect, a sufficient natural wall for the town's defence. But is is thought that a track ran right round the edge of the rock – on which, as has been mentioned, it was never permitted to build houses – and that a battlemented wall was built along it to enable the town's militia to beat off potential assailants who might have scaled the rock by means of long ladders.

The "Via Nuova", today state highway n° 71, to the south-west of the town, leads into Orvieto through the Porta Pertusa or Porta Romana, which may be seen in the background of the photograph. In the wide plain at the foot of the rock, transversed by the same highway, gardens have been laid out, from which fine panoramic views of the Orvietan countryside can be enjoyed. A large car-park, comprising several storeys, has now been built on the site. An escalator leads up from it to the centre of town. The rock of Orvieto has been subjected to a massive programme of consolidation from 1978 onwards. Later, by a law of 1987, provision was made for the allocation of the necessary funds for the comprehensive restoration, refurbishment and recuperation of the town's most significant monuments. Several hundred billion lire, in all, have been allocated to the project. The funds, apart from ensuring the stability of the rock and its monuments, have undoubtedly helped to enhance the town's tourist appeal. In the eastern part of the Piazza Cahen, a wide terrace overlooks Orvieto Scalo and the railway station below: from here a coun-

Porta Postierla.

try road starts out and passes through the Gate under the bastions of the Fortezza Albornoz. A pleasant walk down to the plain below can be had along this road, which passes the Porta Postierla or Porta della Rocca, a fine Gothic double-arched gateway dating to the late 13th century and built into the walls of the fortress. A 13th century marble statue of Boniface VIII is placed in the niche above. The Piazza Cahen is dominated by the Fortezza dell'Albornoz. This fortress was built by the Pontifical Legate Cardinal Egidio Albornoz at the behest of Pope Innocent VI and on the instructions of the soldier-of-fortune and military engineer Ugoli-

no di Montemarte in 1364. Damaged on several occasions, it was reconstructed immediately after the fall of Orvieto's last republican regime and the final subjection of the town to the Papal State (1450-1457). Its inner buildings later fell into ruins, and its outer ditches were filled in during work on the construction of the funicular railway in 1888. More recently, the interior of the fortress has been laid out as a public park and the walkway round the top of its ramparts restored. From here fine views may be enjoyed of the Paglia Valley with the underlying railway station, the Autostrada del Sole and Bracci's now-disused water-powered funicular, which enters the town through a tunnel dug under the fortress. At the centre of a small public park, which we see to the right on leaving Piazza Cahen on the road leading down to the railway station, are the remains of a tetrastyle Etruscan temple: the so-called Temple of Belvedere. Practically no traces of Etruscan buildings have survived in the inhabited centre of Orvieto, since they tended – temples in particular – to be built over by Roman cult buildings, and later Christian churches. The Temple of Belvedere, or the little that remains of it, is the only one of Orvieto's once-numerous temples to survive.

Its discovery was made casually in 1828 during the construction of the new road leading down the valley.

It was probably built at the beginning of the 5th century B. C. and continued to be used down to the early decades of the 3rd century. Its proportions approximate to those prescribed by Virtruvius: the rule, namely, that of the ten parts a temple should consist of, four should be attributed to the central cella and three to each of the lateral cellae. Investigations of the site continued until proper scientific excavations were carried out in 1925; these revealed not only remains of the temple's foundations, but fragments of the decorative terracottas with which it was faced, including part of the pedimental statues now in the "Claudio Faina" Museum. The temple rested on a podium some 22 metres long and 17 broad to which a still-visible flight of steps led up.

T*he Walls*.

The Temple of Belvedere.
The Fortress of Albornoz.

ORVIETO UNDERGROUND

The soft volcanic tufa, easily quarried and shaped to the requirements of form and space to which the people of Orvieto have wished to adapt it, is the raw material from which the town's houses and palaces have been built, and of which the rock on which it stands is constituted. Over thousands of years a network of caves and shafts has been tunnelled into the rock to respond to the needs of the town's inhabitants: quarries, wells, cisterns, cellars, burial vaults, large caves for working terracotta, for pressing olives and grapes, for storing goods, or as animal stalls, were excavated below the small medieval houses, the big places and gardens.

These extensive underground spaces, which complement and complete what stands on the surface of the town, have long been ignored, but have now been rediscovered and restored to their rightful importance: they have once again become attractions, thanks to the atmosphere which pervades them and the interest attached to them in helping us to understand the history of the day-to-day life of the people of Orvieto, who have inhabited them for thousands of years. Today, some of the most interesting caves (about a thousand in all) have been opened to visitors, accompanied by specialist guides..

More particularly, in the Via della Cava at no. 26, a typical Etruscan well over 26 metres deep, can be inspected, while in the Via della Pace, again at no. 26, there is a fascinating series of caves and underground galleries, some of them undoubtedly Etruscan in origin.

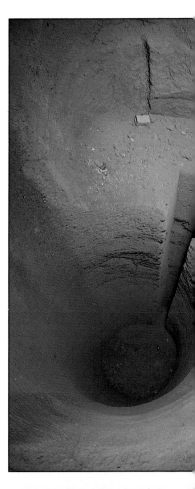

Medieval find of considerable historical interest, discovered and visible by the well known as the Pozzo della Cava. The Etruscan well, an underground chamber thousands of years old and a tunnel linking up with other caves, situated on the Via della Pace.

THE HISTORIC CENTRE OF THE TOWN

In the 14th and 15th century the town of Orvieto was irregularly divided into quarters (*quartieri*), divided in turn into districts (*rioni*). The largest quarter was the one known as Postierla, followed by Santa Pace, San Giovenale and San Giovanni, and Serancia. But during the struggles between the town's two most powerful factions, the "Beffati" and the "Malcorini", many of the unfortified houses were destroyed, the towers demolished, and much of the inhabited area of Orvieto abandoned. At the end of the 15th century, after a long and laborious recovery of civil life, the preceding division of the town was regularized, and the quarters assumed the contours and names they retain to this day. The quarter of Piazza del Popolo (North-East) was called Corsica; that of San Giovenale and San Giovanni, Olmo; that the Postierla (South-East), Santa Maria della Stella; while that of Serancia (South-

Via del Duomo and Torre del Moro.

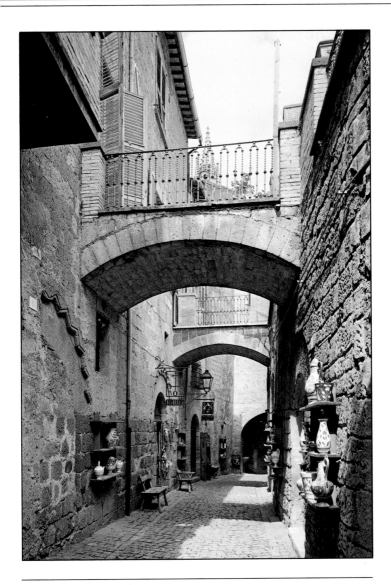

Vicolo dei Dolci.

West) retained its old name. The townscape of Orvieto's historic centre has since then been preserved largely intact, with its narrow, winding streets, often crossed by arches, and flanked by the characteristically low and irregular houses, mainly built out of tufa and basalt, which continuously create interesting perspectives. In the main streets and squares the most conspicuous buldings date to the second half of the 16th century, while in the smaller ones 12-13th century buildings tend to predominate. On leaving the Cathedral, our eyes accustomed to the gloom of its interior, we are momentarily blinded by the brilliant light of the piazza which, in contrast to the Cathedral itself, is rather modest, though well-proportioned, with the squat Torre di Maurizio to the left and the Papal Palace to the right. Then, making our way once again into the dim light of the town's little streets, we may stroll past shops selling souvenirs and the handicraft products for which Orvieto and Umbria are renowned, especially ceramics, terracottas, wood-carvings, wrought iron, and the wines of the area of which the famous white wine of Orvieto is particularly celebrated. To the left of the piazza is the **medieval clock-tower** surmounted by a bronze statue and bell known as the Torre **di Maurizio** after the name of the artist who is thought to have sculpted and cast them in 1351. The statue is 1. 65 m. high and equipped with a hammer with which it strikes the hours on the big bell; the two smaller bells on either side of it are rung each quarter hour by little hammers applied to them. We are now in the **Serancia Quarter** with its many picturesque views. Making our way downhill along the little streets, we may take an interesting stroll along the top of

Via Michelangeli.

Via del Duomo.
Torre di Maurizio.

the town walls.

The Via Cava. This ancient and characteristic street, which leads to the Piazza della Repubblica, divides the medieval **Quarter of Olmo** from that of Serancia. Another view of the Olmo Quarter: houses with elegant mullioned windows, medieval arches and flower-decked balconies. Here we are at the intersection of the Via Ranieri and the Via Ripa di Serancia; a few steps beyond the archway bring us to the church of San Giovanni, from the piazza in front of which we may admire beautiful panoramic views of the rock and surrounding hills. In 1567, on the commission of Monaldo di Cornelio Clementini, the young architect Ippolito Scalza began began work on the building of what was to be the finest mansion-house of the second half of the century in Orvieto, with a beautiful portal and three orders of pedimented windows. Better known as the **Palazzo del Cornelio**, it is situated in the Piazza Ippolito Scalza. The ground floor now houses the municipal "Luigi Fumi" Library, with holdings of 75,000 books, while the upper floors have been turned into a state secondary school. The **Palazzo Michelangeli** on the Via Malabranca (n° 22) has a particularly handsome inner courtyard. Its elegant arcading is supported by basalt columns with a loggia above, exemplifying the choicest forms of the early Renaissance style in Orvieto. One of its rooms also retains delicate late-19th century frescoes framed in magnificent stuccoes, as well as a fine terracotta-tiled floor and stuccoed ceiling. It was in this building, in 1532, that the Simoncelli family of Orvieto – after whom the Palazzo was originally named – acted as hosts to Caterina di Lorenzo de' Medici, future Queen of France.

Quartiere Serancia - Via Cava.

Palazzo del Cornelio.
Palazzo Petrangeli - Courtyard.

The facade and the left-hand side of the Cathedral in an unusual and distinctive view, glimpsed from the Maurizio Tower. As mentioned before, the mediaeval

Torre di Maurizio stands on the left of the Cathedral Square at the corner of Via del Duomo. The original feature of this tower lies in its antique clock and

the statue of Maurizio, named after the artist who, it is said, sculpted and cast it in 1351. The statue, made of bronze, is 1,65 m high and has a hammer which strikes a large bell to signal the hour. The two small bells, on either side of the large one, are fitted with small hammers which strike the quarters.

THE FEAST OF THE PALOMBELLA

Against the picturesque backdrop of its piazzas and buildings, Orvieto is the scene each year of interesting cultural and religious events, such as the Feast of Corpus Christi, the Feast of the Palombella, that of the "Vergine Assunta". The Feast of the Palombella was instituted by the noble lady Giovanna Monaldeschi della Cervara and is celebrated in the Piazza del Duomo at midday on the day of Pentecost (Whit Sunday). A tabernacle in the Gothic style with figures of Mary and the Apostles is placed on the steps in front of the central portal of the Cathedral. This tabernacle is a faithful copy of the wonderful 14th century reliquary of San Savino, the work of the Sienese goldsmiths Ugolino di Vieri and Viva di Lando, which is preserved in the Cathedral Museum. A shrine representing the Empyrean is placed over the lantern of the Church of San Francesco, which is situated on the Via Maitani opposite the Cathedral. A wire is streched from the Empyrean down to the scene of Pentecost in the tabernacle in front of the Cathedral, and, at midday, after the Bishop has given the order to the "master mason" of the Cathedral Fabric to set off the fireworks, a white dove with wings outspread slides swiftly down it, amid loud bangs and clouds of smoke, to the tabernacle, where it triggers off the explosion of other fireworks and lights up little flames over the heads of the Virgin and the Apostles at prayer. Until a few years ago, people drew good or bad omens for the farm year from the outcome of the ceremony. The dove, according to an ancient tradition, is offered by the Bishop to the latest bride in the town. For some time the Feast of the Palombella was held inside the Cathedral, but, in accordance with the provisions of the Lateran Roman Council, was transferred to the piazza outside in 1846.

THE FEAST OF CORPUS CHRISTI - "The Historical Procession"

The Feast of Corpus Christi is celebrated with particular solemnity in Orvieto, in terms of both its historical and religious aspects. It was after the Miracle of Bolsena in 1263 that Pope Urban IV, by his famous Bull "Transiturus", instituted the feast of Corpus Christi in Orvieto on 11 August 1264. Together with numerous cardinals and prelates, and a large concourse of the faithful, Urban IV had already participated in a solemn procession on 19 June, in which the sacred Corporal marked with the blood of Christ – the famous Eucharistic relic of the Miracle of Bolsena – was borne through the streets of the town. Since that day, the Corporal of the Miracle of Bolsena, enshrined in Ugolino

Vieri's magnificent reliquary, has been borne in procession each year, passing through every quarter of Orvieto and all the most important points in the town. For some years now, the procession has been proceded by an important historical procession consisting of some 300 representatives of the various quarters in colourful medieval costumes reproducing – faithful in every detail – the magistrates, captains, standard-bearers and knights of the communal period, and the coats-of-arms of the noble families of Orvieto, and offering an unforgettable spectacle against the background of the medieval and Renaissance city. On the evening of the 14 August, the vigil of

the Feast of the Assumption of the Virgin, ancient protectress of the town, another procession of very ancient origins takes place. In 1338 the general council of Orvieto passed a resolution calling for the statue of the Madonna Assunta to be borne in procession from the church of Sant'Andrea to the Cathedral on the evening before the feast of the Assumption on 15 August, so that the Virgin might liberate the town from the prolonged siege from which it had been suffering.

Standards of the Guilds.

The standard bearers of the Quarters on leaving the Cathedral.
The Reliquary of the Corporal of the Miracle of Bolsena leaving the Cathedral to begin the solemn procession which will wind its way through the streets of the town.

ORVIETO'S HANDICRAFTS AND AGRICULTURE

The art of pottery in Orvieto dates back to the 13th century: the period in which the first products of Umbrian ceramics are identifiable. The pottery style of this period is called "archaic" and derives its inspiration from Orvieto's previous culture, from that of Etruria onwards, combined with intrusive elements of Hispano-Moresque pottery. These initial influences were successively absorbed, developed and surmounted by the local potters, thus giving rise to a particular Orvietan style. During the second half of the 13th century, Orvietan pottery, at first limited to simple wares for everyday usage, became enriched with another fundamental element: white glazing by means of tin oxide; this enabled designs and colours to achieve greater prominence and led to a greater decorative enrichment. From the early years of the 15th century Orvietan pottery attained the height of its artistic expression with the introduction of plastic elements, such as pine-cones, small heads, figures of quadruped animals, real and chimeric coats-of-arms. At the end of the 19th century there was a revival of the art of pottery in Orvieto, modelled on traditional decorative canons. Finds made at the bottom of wells, or in the rubbish dumps of houses great and small, have, since 1906, led to a rediscovery of this medieval pottery, which had hitherto been unknown and which was undoubtedly at the forefront of the ceramics of Central Italy: plates or fragments of plates, jugs and magnificent cups in a perfect state of conservation have thus been brought back to light. And the archaeological evidence has been such that it has been possible to reconstruct the chronological succession of types as mentioned above, and plot changes in technique and artistic form. Already by 1316 Orvietan potters had their own guild which, like the other 23 guilds established under the popular Commune, had its seal impressed on the Bell of the People on top of the Torre del Moro.

Students at work in the pottery workshop of Orvieto's famed Arts and Crafts School.

THE WINE OF ORVIETO

Orvieto is surrounded by an extensive agricultural region formed by a main valley floor corresponding to the basin of the river Paglia, a tributary of the Tiber. The valley is flanked by a rolling countryside of hills clothed in trees, cypresses und vineyards, with the farmhouses of the peasants dotted here and there over the slopes and the square fields alternating with stretches of wood or scrubland. The symbol of this climate is the olive-tree which adorns all the hills of the area up to an altitude of 500 metres or more and is accompanied by cypresses and vines. But the most notable product of the land today is wine: with the abandonment of mixed farming, the landscape is changing its character – share-cropping is giving way to large modern farms and

regular vineyards laid out in rows, which in the space of a few years have substantially increased wine production. The quality of the product, too, has been improved, so much so that it has been given official D.O.C. (Denominazione di Origine Controllata) or *appellation contrôlée* status, which certifies and guarantees its quality and distinction. The soil from which this wine comes, mainly consisting of clays and sands covered by volcanic material, the mild climate favourable to the ripening of the grapes and the excellent exposure of the hillslopes, are all fundamental factors that have concurred to give Orvieto wine its high quality. Today, the old peasant systems of cultivation are gradually being ousted by more modern and remunerative methods. Better equipped and more functional wine cellars are likewise to be found alongside the old picturesque cellars dug out of the tufa in which the "Orvieto" is fermented and matured in enormous oak casks before being bottled and marketed throughout the world. The "Orvieto" exists in two versions, dry (*secco*) and sweetish (*abboccato*), both obtained by a mixture of grapes from the following vines. Trebbiano Tosano, Verdello, Sacchetto, Drupeggio and Malvasia Toscana. Straw yellow in colour, it is a wine of a pleasant flowery bouquet, with an alcohol content of approximately 11° – 12°, and a clean fresh teste rather similar to that of fresh grapes.

The wine of Orvieto, well-known since the time of the Etruscans, is one of the most ancient wines of Italy. During the Renaissance it graced the table of illustrious popes, cardinals and princes. It was particularly appreciated by Luca Signorelli who, by the contract drawn up between him and the Chamberlain of the Cathedral Board of Works on 27 April 1500 for the decoration of the Chapel of San Brizio, obtained: «375 ducats, a house with two beds, two bushels of wheat per month and 12 some (1 soma = ca. 145 litres) of wine per year», i. e. well over a thousand litres!

The tourist who arrives in Orvieto and leaves his car in the new "Porta Romana" car-park can immediately admire the gentle landscape of the surrounding countryside; a little road flanked by cypresses clambering up the hillside and ancient pathways, one of which leads to the ancient Convent of the Capuchins.

THE ENVIRONS OF ORVIETO

Prodo, Turreted Castle dating to the 14th century.
Castel Viscardo, the 14th century Castle.
Opposite: Alviano - The Castle.
The dam and lake of Corbara.

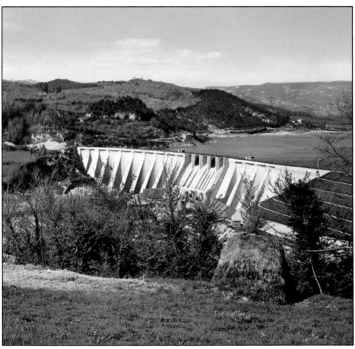

USEFUL TOURIST INFORMATION

Emergencies	tel. 113
Town Hall	tel. 342225
Carabinieri	tel. 41955
Traffic Police	tel. 300158
The Police	tel. 342476
Traffic wardens	tel. 340088

Taxi - Piazza della Repubblica
tel. 342613

Taxi - Orvieto Scalo	tel. 90303
Railway station	tel. 90034

Hospital S. Maria Stella
tel. 3091

Red cross	tel. 341727
Fire brigate	tel. 90666

A.C.I. - Breakdown recovery
service tel. 90282

Tourist Information
Board
Piazza del Duomo
tel.341772-341911 - Fax 344433

MUSEUMS

Duomo - Sagrestia
Piazza del Duomo tel. 341167

Museo dell'Opera del Duomo
Piazza del Duomo tel. 342477

Museo Emilio Greco
Piazza del Duomo - Palazzo
Soliano tel. 344605

Museo Archeologico Claudio
Faina e Civico
Piazza del Duomo - Palazzo
Faina tel. 341216

Necropoli Etrusca
Ss.71 km16 tel. 343611

Pozzo di San Patrizio
Viale San Gallo tel. 343768

Orvieto Underground tel. 344891

Pozzo della Cava
Via della Cava tel. 342373

Torre del Moro
Corso Cavour tel. 344567

HOTELS ORVIETO CENTRO STORICO

* * * *

Aquila Bianca
Via Garibaldi 13 tel. 341246

Maitani
Via Maltani 5 tel. 342011

* * *

Filippeschi
Via Filippeschi 19 tel. 343275

Italia
Via di Piazza del Popolo 13
tel. 342065

Reale
Piazza del Popolo 25 tel. 341247

Valentino
Via A. da Orvieto 32 tel. 342464

Virgilio
Piazza del Duomo 5 tel. 343797

* *

Corso
Corso Cavour 343 tel. 342020

Duomo
Via Maurizio 7 tel. 341887

Della Posta
Via Signorelli 18 tel. 341909

Hotels Orvieto Scalo

* * *

La Badia
(con ristorante)
Abbazia dei SS. Severo
e Martirio   tel. 90359

Etruria
Via Costanzi 104   tel. 90207

Europa
Via Gramsci 2   tel. 90771

Gialletti
(con ristorante)
Via Costanzi 71   tel. 90381

Kristal
Via Costanzi 69   tel. 90703

Orvieto
Via Costanzi 65   tel. 91751

Villa Ciconia
(con ristorante)
Via dei Tigli 29   tel. 92982

* *

Paradiso
(con ristorante)
Via 7 Martiri 49   tel. 90294

La Pergoletta
Via dei Sette Martiri 3
                        tel. 301418

Umbria
(con ristorante)
Via Monte Nibbio 1/3
                        tel. 90340

*

Centrale
Via 7 Martiri   tel. 93281

Picchio
Via Salvatori 17   tel. 90246

Primavera
Strada dell'Arcone 2/6
                        tel. 341781

Restaurants Orvieto

Al Pozzo Etrusco
Piazza de' Ranieri 1   tel. 344456

Al San Francesco
Via Maitani 15   tel. 43302

Antico Bucchero
Via de' Cartari 4   tel. 341725

**Cantina Ottaviani
Duca di Orvieto**
Via della Pace 26   tel. 344663

Dell'Ancora
Via di Piazza del Popolo 9
                        tel. 342766

Del Cocco
Via Garibaldi 6   tel. 342319

Il Giglio d'Oro
Piazza Duomo 8   tel. 341903

I Sette Consoli
Piazza S. Angelo 1   tel. 343911

La Buca
C.so Cavour 299   tel. 344792

L'Antica Rupe
Via Sant'Antonio 2/A   tel. 343063

Le Grotte del Funaro
Via Ripa Serancia 41   tel. 343276

Maurizio
Via Duomo 78   tel. 341114

San Giovenale
Piazza San Giovenale 6
                        tel. 340642

Taverna dell'Etrusco
Via della Misericordia 5
                        tel. 43947

Black Out
Corso Cavour 310   tel. 340873

INDEX

Fotografie: Archivio Plurigraf - Barone
Foto pag. 48/49 gentilmente concesse dalla "Fondazione per il Museo Claudio Faina"
Le foto aeree concess. S.M.A. 506 del 20/06/1991